{geography focus}

CHANGING CLIMATE

{living with the weather}

Louise Spilsbury

www.raintreepublishers.co.uk

Visit our website to find out more information about **Raintree** books.

To order:

 Phone 44 (0) 1865 888112

Send a fax to 44 (0) 1865 314091

 Visit the Raintree Bookshop at **www.raintreepublishers.co.uk** to browse our catalogue and order online.

First published 2006 by Heinemann Library a division of Harcourt Education Australia, 20 Thackray Road, Port Melbourne Victoria 3207 Australia (a division of Reed International Books Australia Pty Ltd, ABN 70 001 002 357). Visit the Heinemann Library website at www.heinemannlibrary.com.au

Published in Great Britain in 2006 by Raintree, Halley Court, Jordan Hill, Oxford OX2 8EJ, part of Harcourt Education www.raintreepublishers.co.uk

 A Reed Elsevier company

Editorial: Moira Anderson, Carmel Heron, Diyan Leake, Patrick Catel
Cover, text design & graphs: Marta White
Photo research: Karen Forsythe, Wendy Duncan
Production: Tracey Jarrett, Duncan Gilbert
Map diagrams: Guy Holt
Technical diagrams: Nives Porcellato & Andy Craig

Typeset in 12/17.5 pt Gill Sans Regular
Origination by Modern Age
Printed and bound in Hong Kong, China by South China Printing Company Ltd

The paper used to print this book comes from sustainable resources.

National Library of Australia Cataloguing-in-Publication data:

Spilsbury, Louise.
    Changing climate : living with the weather.

    Includes index.
    For upper primary and lower secondary school students.
    ISBN 1 74070 275 1.

    1. Climatic changes – Juvenile literature.
    2. Weather – Juvenile literature. 3. Global warming – Juvenile literature. 1. Title. (Series : Spilsbury, Louise. Geography focus).

551.6

Acknowledgements

The publisher would like to thank the following for permission to reproduce copyright material: Age Fotostock: p. **10**; APL/Corbis/ Ariel Skelley: p. **4**; Dinodia Photo Library/Sham D. Manchekar: p. **26**; Dr John Day: p. **20**; Lonely Planet Images/Dennis Johnson: p. **18**, /Richard l'Anson: p. **8**, /Chris Mellor: p. **14**; NASA: p. **41** (upper & lower); Newspix: p. **39**; PhotoDisc: pp. **24** (left & right), **28, 32, 40**; PhotoEdit Inc./Bob Daemmrich: p. **12**; Photolibrary.com: p. **45**, /Bill Alexander: p. **38**, /Images Agence Photographique: p. **22**, /Index Stock: p. **9**, /Mauritius Die Bildagentur: p. **17**, /OSF: pp. **6, 30**, /Science Photo Library: pp. **42–43**; Reuters/Picture Media/Carlos Barria: p. **34**; StockXchange: p. **44**. All other images PhotoDisc.

Cover photograph of the ocean reproduced with permission of PhotoDisc; inset photograph of flooding in Bangladesh reproduced with permission of Getty Images/AFP.

Every attempt has been made to trace and acknowledge copyright. Where an attempt has been unsuccessful, the publisher would be pleased to hear from the copyright owner so any omission or error can be rectified.

Disclaimer

All the Internet addresses (URLs) given in this book were valid at the time of going to press. However, due to the dynamic nature of the Internet, some addresses may have changed, or sites may have changed or ceased to exist since publication. While the author and publishers regret any inconvenience this may cause readers, no responsibility for any such changes can be accepted by either the author or the publishers.

{contents}

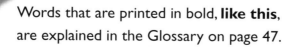

Words that are printed in bold, **like this**,
are explained in the Glossary on page 47.

{the world's weather}

People have always talked about the weather. In ancient times, many people believed that storms and sunshine were controlled by the gods. They would try to find ways of keeping the gods happy to prevent bad weather. Today we understand how the weather works but it is still a major topic of conversation because it has a huge impact on all our lives. Weather is not a static thing – weather can change from day to day and some scientists think that even bigger changes are happening. To understand these changes you first need to know about how weather and **climates** work.

Weather and climate

The sunshine, clouds, rain, or wind we see outside are part of the day's weather. The climate of a place is the pattern of weather that has happened there for many years. For example, Australia's climate includes hot, dry summers.

Weather affects what people do. What different things can you do in the snow?

World climate zones

This map shows how the world's major climates are found in five bands, or zones, around the Earth. Scientists worked out the zones using averages of the temperature and the amount of rain each place experienced every month and every year.

The five climate types are **tropical**, dry, **temperate**, cool, and polar.

1 Tropical climates have high temperatures all year round and get a large amount of rain.

2 Dry climates have very little rain and are hot most of the year.

3 Temperate climates are moderate in rainfall and temperature. They often have distinct seasonal changes in moisture and temperature levels.

4 Cool climates have severe winters and mild or warm summers. They may be generally humid or very dry.

5 Polar climates are found in places that have freezing temperatures for most of the year.

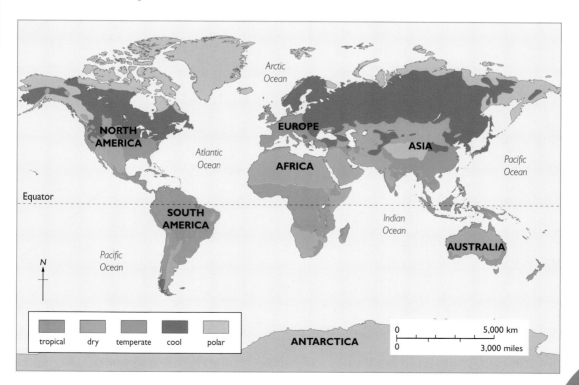

World climate zones: Which one do you live in?

{climates and living things}

Have you ever thought about why one part of the world is covered in dry, sandy desert, and another has lush, green rainforests? **Biomes** are different kinds of natural landscapes and the living things within them. **Climate** is the main reason biomes are different from each other.

Creating biomes

Differences in climate have a huge effect on plant and animal life in an area. In areas with a very hot and dry climate, desert biomes may form. Animals and plants that live in deserts have features that enable them to survive the heat and lack of rain. Desert plants such as cactuses survive dry times by storing water in their swollen stems. These stems also have spikes that stop thirsty animals breaking into them. Desert animals include camels that can go without water for several days, and lizards that have a thick skin that protects them from the burning sun.

Desert biomes have particular kinds of plants and animals because they are suited to the climate there.

Plants need water and warmth to grow well and rainforests flourish in **tropical** climates. Rainforests are home to giant trees, lush ferns, and climbing plants. These plants and the fruit, nuts, and seeds they produce provide food for a vast range of animal life. Rainforest animals feed either on the plants or on the animals that eat the plants.

FACT!

Cold areas covered with coniferous forest are also known as taiga. This is the biggest type of biome of all, because taiga covers nearly one-fifth of all the land in the world.

Biomes of the world

This map shows some of the world's major biomes. When you have had a good look at it, turn back to page 5 and compare it to the climate map there. You should be able to spot the way climate determines which biomes develop where.

Rainforests form in the tropical zones. Grasslands, bare land with large areas of grass and patches of other plants, and deserts form in the dry zones. **Broadleaf woodlands**, with trees such as oak and beech, grow in **temperate** zones. **Coniferous forest**, with pine and fir trees, is found in cool zones. The areas marked 'treeless' are where the land is frozen and only a few kinds of plants, such as lichens and moss, can grow.

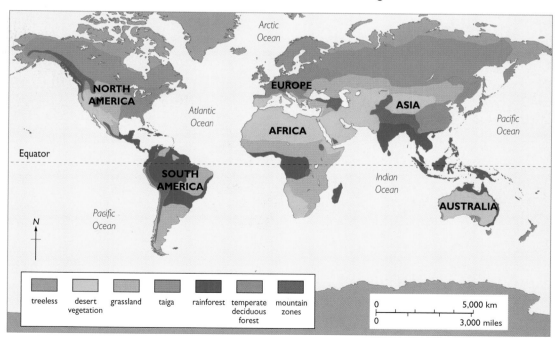

This map shows the world's major biomes.

{people and weather}

The different kinds of weather around the world have an impact on many aspects of people's lives. Weather affects the jobs they do, the sports they play, what people wear, and what their houses look like.

Farmers and fishermen listen to the information about the weather that is given out in **weather forecasts**. Fishing boats may not be able to set out in a storm. Farmers may have to bring livestock inside if snow or storms are forecast. In some places there are special forecasts for sports players to tell them if weather conditions are right for play. And how many of us look out of the window to check if it is cold or warm, wet or windy before we decide what clothes to wear each day?

Weather and moods

Feeling blue? Blame the weather! The cold, dusty Mistral wind that blows through the Rhone Valley in France is said to make people irritable.

Many people travel round the world to enjoy different climates. People go on holiday to places like the Mediterranean (above) to enjoy the hot, sunny climate.

Houses and homes

Today people can control the temperatures in their houses. We have central heating to make homes warm in cold countries and air conditioning to cool houses in hot places. However, around the world you can still see differences in houses built to suit different **climates**.

People who live in places with very wet climates may get floods, when water covers the land. They sometimes build their houses on stilts, to raise them above the water level. In cold places, people build houses with thick walls and double-glazed windows to keep out cold air and keep in warm air. In hot climates, windows may be large and open to let air through or slatted so they can be partly closed to keep the burning sun out. On some Greek islands, house walls are painted white. White is a colour that reflects sunlight away from the walls and stops them getting too hot.

These colourful houses are in Norway, a country that gets heavy snowfall. The steep sloping roofs allow the snow to slide off. If snow piled up on the roofs, they would collapse.

{the atmosphere}

The **atmosphere** is the key to all the different kinds of weather in our world. The atmosphere is a blanket of gases that wrap around the Earth, rather like the layer of peel around an orange. These gases are held in place by gravity, the force that pulls things towards the Earth. The atmosphere protects the Earth from some of the intense heat given off by the Sun and makes it possible for us all to live in our world without being burned up. The atmosphere is made up of four layers. The Earth's weather all happens in the lowest part of the atmosphere – the **troposphere**.

Air pressure

The force that the atmosphere puts on any object is called **air pressure**. Since the atmosphere is created by the attraction of gases to the Earth due to gravity, air nearer to the Earth is denser than air further away. This denser air causes pressures near the surface to be higher than pressures further up, where the air is less dense or thinner.

Inside aeroplanes the cabins have raised air pressure. This is because the air pressure high in the atmosphere would be too thin for people to breathe.

What makes up the atmosphere?

This diagram shows the four layers of air in the atmosphere. The air is made up of gases, mainly nitrogen, some **oxygen**, which we need to breathe, and small amounts of **carbon dioxide** and other gases.

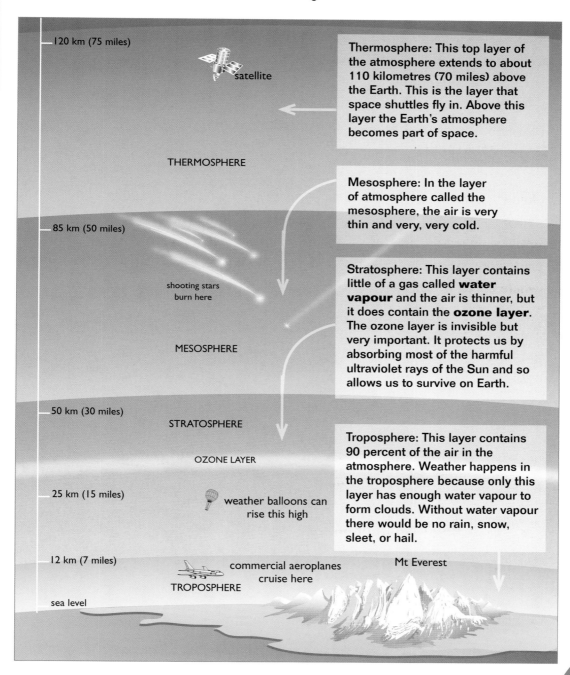

120 km (75 miles)

satellite

THERMOSPHERE

Thermosphere: This top layer of the atmosphere extends to about 110 kilometres (70 miles) above the Earth. This is the layer that space shuttles fly in. Above this layer the Earth's atmosphere becomes part of space.

Mesosphere: In the layer of atmosphere called the mesosphere, the air is very thin and very, very cold.

85 km (50 miles)

shooting stars burn here

MESOSPHERE

Stratosphere: This layer contains little of a gas called **water vapour** and the air is thinner, but it does contain the **ozone layer**. The ozone layer is invisible but very important. It protects us by absorbing most of the harmful ultraviolet rays of the Sun and so allows us to survive on Earth.

50 km (30 miles)

STRATOSPHERE

OZONE LAYER

Troposphere: This layer contains 90 percent of the air in the atmosphere. Weather happens in the troposphere because only this layer has enough water vapour to form clouds. Without water vapour there would be no rain, snow, sleet, or hail.

25 km (15 miles)

weather balloons can rise this high

12 km (7 miles)

commercial aeroplanes cruise here

Mt Everest

TROPOSPHERE

sea level

The layers of the atmosphere.

{sunshine}

The Sun is the energy source that powers the world's weather. The heat energy that it sends out warms the **atmosphere**. Warmth from the Sun passes to Earth through the atmosphere. The Earth then gives off warmth. This is then trapped by the atmosphere. The atmosphere acts as a blanket around the Earth, trapping its own heat, the way that a jacket keeps you warm by trapping the heat you give off.

FACT!

The Sun is our nearest star. It is a huge ball of boiling gases, over 100 times bigger than Earth. The Sun is 150 million kilometres (94 million miles) away but it provides our planet with all its heat and light.

The light and heat that reach us from the Sun are very strong. That is why we should all cover up and put on sunblock to avoid getting sunburnt. On sunny days you lose water from your body when you sweat. You need to keep your body topped up with water, so make sure you drink plenty.

Why are some places hotter than others?

Some places on Earth are hotter than others because they get different amounts of the Sun's heat. This is because the Earth is shaped like a ball and has a curved surface. The Sun's rays travel to Earth in straight lines, but because the Earth is curved the rays hit the land at different angles. The rays hit the **Equator**, an imaginary line around the centre of the Earth, most directly. That is why the Equator is the hottest part of the planet. The Sun's rays hit the North Pole and South Pole at a very slanting angle so the heat is spread out over a much wider area.

The average temperatures of a place also vary because of other factors. For example, mountaintops are cold even in warm countries because the air in the **troposphere** gets colder the higher you go. The temperature of an area is also affected by how close it is to an ocean. Places near the sea are slightly cooler than average in summer and warmer than average in winter because land cools down and heats up more quickly near the sea.

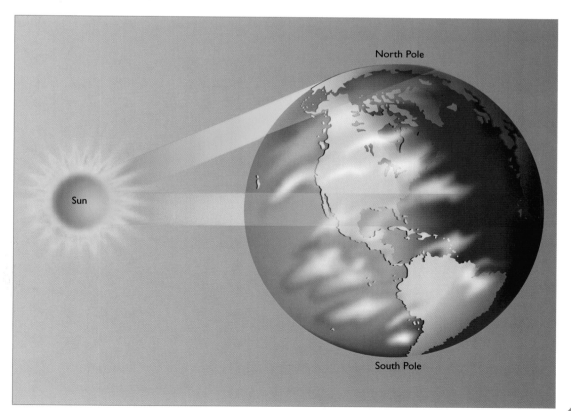

The Sun's rays hitting Earth.

{why do winds blow?}

Wind is moving air, whether it takes the form of a gentle breeze or a howling gale. Air gets the energy it needs to move from the Sun. The Sun warms different parts of the air, and because warm air is lighter than cold air, it rises up in the **atmosphere**. Cooler air flows into the gaps where the warm air has risen from. These air movements are winds.

High and low pressure

You have probably heard **weather forecasters** talk about areas of high and low pressure. In general, cool air creates areas of **high pressure** because it is heavier than warm air. This causes it to sink and press down more heavily on the Earth. When warm air rises, it creates an area of **low pressure** because in these areas the air is pressing less heavily on Earth. The greater the difference between the high pressure and low pressure in a particular place, the greater the speed of the winds there.

This sailboat catches wind in its sails to move.

A world of winds

Winds blow around the world in fairly predictable patterns because there are bands of high and low pressure around the Earth. There is always an area of high pressure around the North Pole and South Pole because they are the coldest places on Earth. The **Equator** is the hottest place on Earth and there is always a band of low pressure here. Winds blow because air always tries to move from areas of high pressure to areas of low pressure.

When warm air rises above the Equator, it is replaced by cooler air from the North and South Poles. However, the Earth is constantly spinning on its axis, an imaginary line that goes through the centre of the Earth. The spinning movement sends these winds off-course. Instead of flowing north and south, the winds are blown left and right and this is how we get westerly and easterly winds.

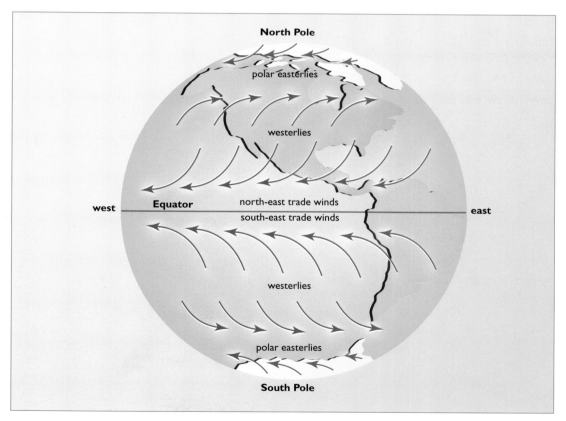

The winds that blow from the east above and below the Equator are known as **trade winds**. *They got their name from the time when huge sailing ships criss-crossed the oceans to buy and sell goods – to trade – and used the winds to speed them along.*

{rain}

We might grumble when it rains, but rain is vitally important to our planet. It fills our rivers and lakes with the water that plants and all other living things, including humans, need to live. Rain falls in almost every part of the world, but in very different amounts. In some places there are frequent **droughts**. These are periods of low rainfall when it may rain only once in a year. In some places, rain can fall very heavily over a short period of time and this can cause floods.

How does rain form?

Rain falls because the water forming raindrops is part of the **water cycle** (see diagram below). When the Sun warms water on the land and at the surface of the ocean, some of it **evaporates**. That means it turns from liquid water into **water vapour**, a gas in the air.

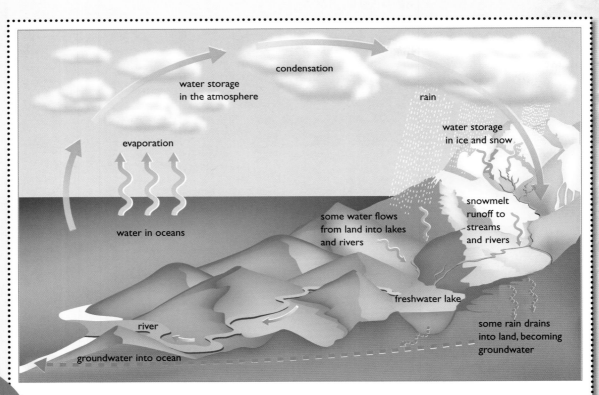

Rain is part of the water cycle.

When this warm vapour gets higher in the air, it cools down. Cool air cannot hold as much water vapour as warm air, so the extra water vapour turns back into very tiny droplets of water. This is called **condensation**. When millions of these droplets gather together, they form clouds. These droplets move around in clouds and bump into each other. As they do so, they join together and become raindrops. When these raindrops are big and heavy enough, gravity makes them fall from the sky down to Earth again.

Snow and hail

Rain, snow, and hail are all forms of **precipitation** – water falling from the sky in liquid or solid form. Snow consists of tiny crystals of ice that stick together. Hail usually forms in large thunderclouds, where balls of ice are repeatedly pulled far up into the cold parts of the **atmosphere**. On each trip upwards, a new layer of ice freezes to the outside of the hailstone. Finally, the hailstone becomes so heavy that it falls to the ground.

Snow forms when droplets of water vapour freeze into tiny pieces of ice called particles. The ice particles get bigger and become ice crystals. The ice crystals join to become snowflakes.

{clouds}

Clouds do not only form from water that **evaporates** from the land or sea. The clouds that hide mountain peaks are formed in a different way. A damp wind blows towards a mountain and gets forced upwards by the slope. When the wind reaches the cold air around the mountaintop, the **water vapour** within it **condenses** and forms clouds.

Clouds also form when a band of warm air meets a band of cold air, because the warm air gets pushed upwards. When this warm air gets high and cold enough, the water vapour condenses into a cloud.

Jet aeroplanes fly high above the Earth in the stratosphere. Here the air is still and you can look down on the clouds.

Mists and fog

Fog is cloud that forms near the ground or over the sea. When fog is so thin you can see through it, we call it mist. Fog and mist form when warm, damp air cools down and the water condenses on tiny particles (bits) of dust in the air.

Kinds of clouds

There are three main types of cloud: cirrus, cumulus, and stratus. Different clouds bring different amounts of rainfall, and some clouds are actually signs of good weather.

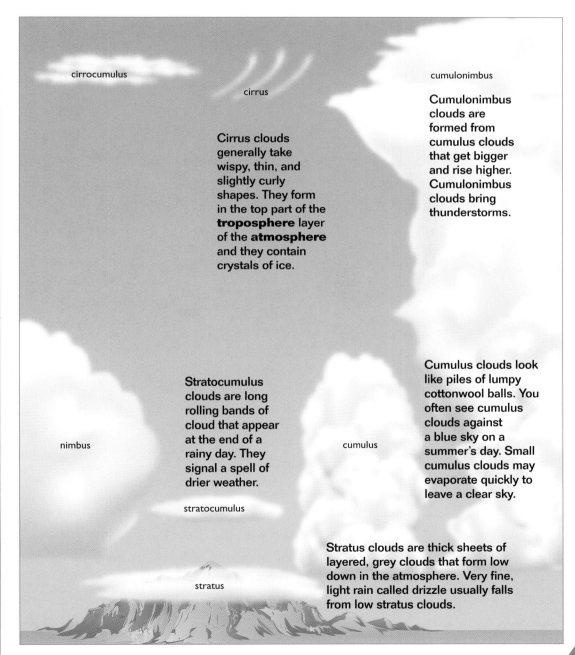

cirrocumulus

cirrus

Cirrus clouds generally take wispy, thin, and slightly curly shapes. They form in the top part of the troposphere layer of the atmosphere and they contain crystals of ice.

cumulonimbus

Cumulonimbus clouds are formed from cumulus clouds that get bigger and rise higher. Cumulonimbus clouds bring thunderstorms.

nimbus

Stratocumulus clouds are long rolling bands of cloud that appear at the end of a rainy day. They signal a spell of drier weather.

stratocumulus

cumulus

Cumulus clouds look like piles of lumpy cottonwool balls. You often see cumulus clouds against a blue sky on a summer's day. Small cumulus clouds may evaporate quickly to leave a clear sky.

Stratus clouds are thick sheets of layered, grey clouds that form low down in the atmosphere. Very fine, light rain called drizzle usually falls from low stratus clouds.

stratus

Different kinds of cloud can mix to form other kinds of cloud.

{what are weather fronts?}

A weather front is the dividing line between a mass of warm air and a mass of cold air. The two kinds of air in a weather front mingle in a series of swirls because the Earth is spinning on its **axis**. These swirls of air are known as depressions. When different air masses meet, the warm air rises and the colder air **condenses** and forms clouds and rain. When you hear a **weather forecaster** talking about weather fronts, it usually means rain is on the way.

Warm fronts

A warm front is where a band of warm air catches up with a band of colder air. Warm air rises slowly over the cooler air because warm air is lighter. This means that clouds form slowly over a large area and often bring a long period of drizzle. The rain continues until the warm front has passed over. A warm front is always in front of the cold front.

Wispy clouds like this mean that a warm front is on its way.

Cold fronts

A cold front forms when cold air meets warm air. At a cold front, cold air slides below the warm air and so forces the warm air to rise more quickly. Because the air is cooled quickly at a cold front, a narrow band of thick cumulonimbus clouds forms. These dark clouds bring bursts of heavy rain.

Occluded fronts

Cold fronts usually move more quickly than warm fronts. Where a cold front catches up with a warm front we call it an occluded front. At an occluded front, the cold air pushes the warm air up into the **atmosphere**. In the higher atmosphere, the warm air cools, condenses, and forms bursts of very heavy rain.

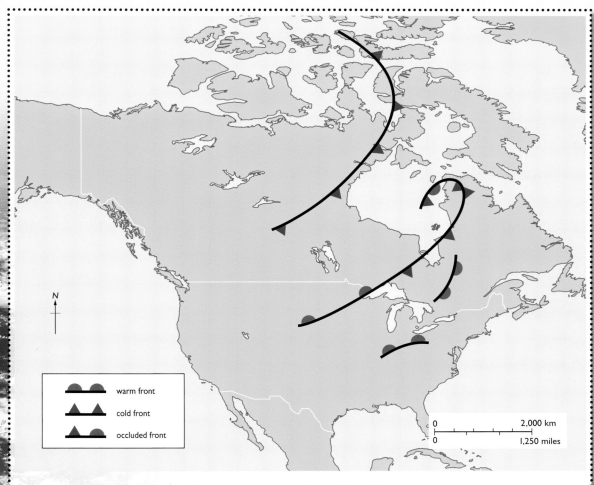

On a weather map, a warm front is shown by a line with half moon shapes on it. A cold front is shown by a line with triangles on it.

21

{thunder and lightning}

We all know that a large, dark-grey cloud in the sky means it is going to rain. Rain clouds look dark because they are so full of **water vapour** that the sunshine cannot pass through them. Thunderstorms that bring heavy rain, loud thunderclaps, and flashes of lightning come from cumulonimbus clouds, the dark giants of the sky.

Cumulonimbus clouds develop from cumulus clouds that get bigger as they are joined by masses of rising warm air. They extend from low down up to 15 kilometres (9 miles) above ground. Cumulonimbus clouds bring heavy rain because the tiny droplets of water blow around inside them, colliding and joining to form ever-larger drops.

FACT!

Over 500 million litres (100 million gallons) of rain can fall from a single thunderstorm – that is enough water to fill 2,000 Olympic-sized swimming pools.

Lightning can be dangerous, so get inside if you see it coming.
Never stand under trees outside because they attract lightning.

How do thunderclouds work?

High winds build up inside cumulonimbus thunderclouds. These high winds can reach speeds of 200 kilometres (125 miles) an hour. When ice and water particles are blown about this fast in the cloud, they rub and bump together. This friction creates electrical charges and sparks. (This is the same way that people can start a spark for a fire by rubbing two dry sticks together very quickly.)

The upper part of a cumulonimbus cloud has positive electrical charges (shown by a plus symbol in the diagram below). The lower part of the cloud has a negative charge (shown by the minus symbol). The land below the cloud also has positive charges. When clouds develop very large electrical charges, they may release an electric current that flows towards Earth. This is what we see as a flash of forked lightning. A lightning bolt is incredibly hot and it heats up the air around it. The thunder we hear is the noise made when the air in front of the lightning suddenly expands in the heat.

This diagram shows the positive and negative charges in a thundercloud.

{seasons}

In some places the weather is much the same all year round, but in others the changing seasons bring different kinds of weather. For many people, autumn and winter bring fewer hours of sunshine, so the days feel shorter and it gets much colder. In spring and summer there are more hours of sunshine, so the days are warmer and longer. Countries on different parts of the Earth get more and less sunshine at different times of the year because of the angle at which the Earth travels around the Sun.

Wet and dry seasons

Countries such as Australia, the UK, and the USA have cold winter and warm summer seasons. In places close to the **Equator**, the number of hours of sunlight does not change much through the year. It is the amount of rain that varies. In these places people experience a rainy season at a certain time of the year followed by a dry season. In many countries in southern Asia, the rainy season is called the **monsoon**.

FACT!

Because the Earth is tilted on its axis, the North and South Poles get no sunshine for 182 days (over half) of the year.

The changing weather patterns of the different seasons bring changes to trees and plants.

Reasons for the seasons

Seasons happen because the Earth is tilted on an angle at its axis, the imaginary line that goes through its centre from the North to the South Pole. The Earth takes a year to travel around the Sun in a special path in space called an **orbit**. So each place on Earth only spends part of its time facing the Sun. At any one moment, the places facing the Sun are generally warmer than those facing away. However, because the Sun shines more intensely near the Equator than near the Poles, it never gets too warm at the Poles, even during long summer days.

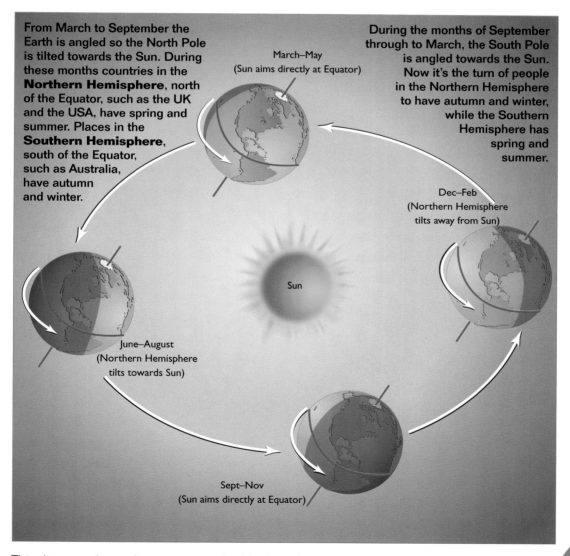

From March to September the Earth is angled so the North Pole is tilted towards the Sun. During these months countries in the **Northern Hemisphere**, north of the Equator, such as the UK and the USA, have spring and summer. Places in the **Southern Hemisphere**, south of the Equator, such as Australia, have autumn and winter.

During the months of September through to March, the South Pole is angled towards the Sun. Now it's the turn of people in the Northern Hemisphere to have autumn and winter, while the Southern Hemisphere has spring and summer.

March–May
(Sun aims directly at Equator)

Dec–Feb
(Northern Hemisphere tilts away from Sun)

Sun

June–August
(Northern Hemisphere tilts towards Sun)

Sept–Nov
(Sun aims directly at Equator)

This diagram shows the seasons in the Northern Hemisphere.

{case study} monsoon in India

When the **monsoon** rains arrive in India in June and July, there are scenes of great rejoicing. People celebrate because the rainy season brings relief from the intense heat that becomes almost unbearable in April and May. They are also happy because fields of crops get the water they need at last and farmers can start planting rice.

What causes the monsoon?

In India and other parts of southern Asia, a **high-pressure** weather system develops for half the year. This is when cool, dry winds blow in from the deserts of Tibet and central Asia.

FACT!

India is the wettest place in the world during the monsoon season, when 25 billion tonnes (28 billion tons) of rain fall each day.

During the monsoon in India, it rains every day, but not all day. There are heavy downpours that fill the streets with water, and then the air clears and sunshine returns.

During the region's hottest months, in April and May, the Sun warms the land and an area of **low pressure** forms above it. Now the winds change direction, blowing in from the southern Indian Ocean and on to the land. These are the **trade winds**. The air is full of **water vapour** that **evaporated** from the warm ocean. As the winds move across India, they release this water in heavy monsoon rains.

Life and death

Although the monsoon rains bring life, they also bring destruction. Every year the sudden, heavy downpours cause rivers to overspill their banks. These floods destroy thousands of homes, roads, and railway lines, and can kill livestock and people.

Monsoon movements

This map shows how the monsoon spreads across southern Asia every year. People there know when the annual monsoon rains are due to arrive in their district almost to the day. The rain comes in steadily, starting in the far south of the country on around 1 June. Over the next six weeks (see the yellow lines) it spreads gradually north-west until it covers the whole of the country by mid-July. The monsoon finally ends in October. The orange arrows show the direction of the trade winds.

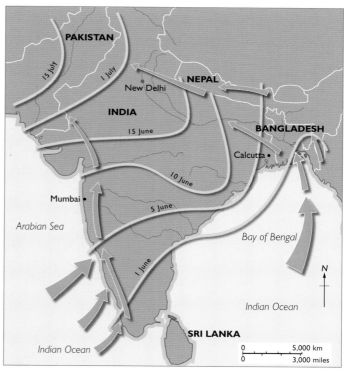

This map shows how warm wet winds blow from the south-west and how the monsoon starts at different times.

{understanding weather forecasts}

Before you set out for a day's cycling, sailing, fishing, or climbing, you probably check the **weather forecast**. Weather forecasts are given out over the radio, TV, Internet, and in newspapers. Many people, including farmers and fishermen, follow forecasts very carefully.

Gathering information

Weather forecasters collect information from **meteorologists** in weather stations all over the world, on land, and at sea. Meteorologists are scientists who study the weather. They use special balloons that float in the air to record **air pressure**, temperature, and **humidity** (amount of moisture in the air). They use containers called rain gauges to collect and measure amounts of rainfall in an area. They measure air pressure with instruments called barometers. Weather forecasters feed all these data into computers and compile charts and maps that show where different weather systems are. From these they can predict where the movements caused by air pressure and winds are likely to take these weather systems next.

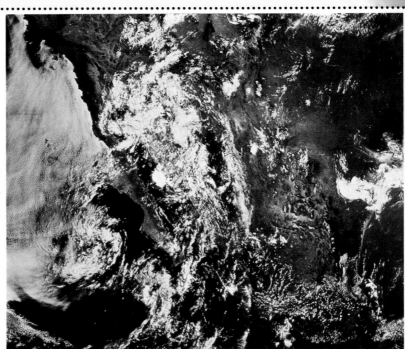

*Weather forecasters use photos like this taken from a **satellite** in space to track cloud size and movements. The brighter a cloud appears, the thicker it is.*

What do weather maps mean?

Weather maps give us information about weather in our area and across the wider world. They tell us about **precipitation**, wind speed, and temperatures.

On this weather map you can see numbers that indicate temperatures given in degrees Centigrade. The curved lines on the map are isobars. They join areas of the same air pressure, either areas of **high pressure** or **low pressure**. This is tricky to understand, but all you really need to remember is that the tighter the isobar lines are together, the stronger the winds. Weather forecasters call close isobar lines 'depressions' because they are linked to areas of low pressure.

The symbols on the map indicate weather types such as rain, sun, and snow. The key beside the map helps you work out what these symbols mean.

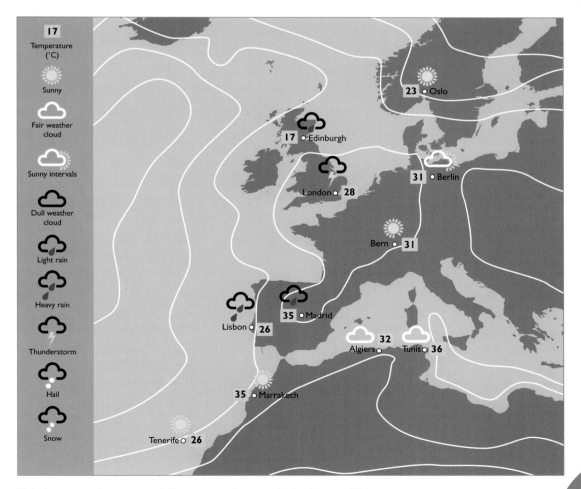

This is a weather map of Europe and part of Northern Africa.

{weather hazards}

Daily **weather forecasts** are usually at the back of a newspaper or shown at the end of a TV news programme, but weather hazards make front-page news. Every year stories of **droughts**, floods, landslides, and hurricanes make the headlines.

Kinds of weather hazards

Floods happen when an unusually large amount of rain falls on an area in a short time, covering a normally dry area of land with water. Rushing water is heavy and can knock down buildings, wash away cars, and drown people and animals. It also causes mud and rock to slip down hillsides, destroying roads and villages. A drought happens when an area that usually gets rain has little or no rain for a long time. Droughts in parts of Africa can last for years and cause terrible suffering. Crops and animals die and people who are not able to buy food or get water may die.

Hailstones can be weather hazards. Large hailstones can cause terrible damage to cars, houses, and crops. They can be the size of a large grapefruit.

El Niño

You may have heard of El Niño on the news. It is often blamed for weather hazards. El Niño is a large, warm ocean current, roughly the size of Europe. It pushes warm water from the waters off the South American coast across the Pacific Ocean to near Australia. Once every two to seven years the **trade winds** that hold the warm water there blow in the opposite direction and carry it back across the Pacific to the South American coast.

This might not sound like a big deal, but the heat that gets trapped in El Niño waters affects air currents in the **atmosphere**. These changes can reverse weather patterns. Normally dry countries become wet, and normally wet ones become dry. The effects of El Niño may last months and cause drought, floods, mudslides, and an increased number of hurricanes.

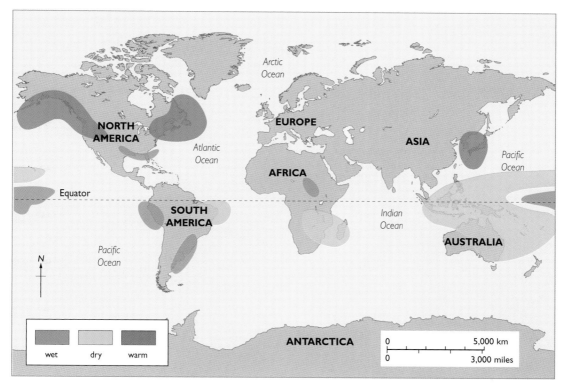

*This world map shows the parts of the world where El Niño regularly affects the **climate**. It makes these areas much wetter, drier, or warmer than normal.*

{what are hurricanes?}

Hurricanes are the most powerful and destructive storms on Earth. They are spiralling, fast winds that start over the sea and hurtle towards coasts. They cause giant waves, blow down buildings, uproot trees, and throw cars and boats about like toys.

How do hurricanes form?

Hurricanes form over **tropical** oceans near the **Equator**, because these areas of water are always very warm. This heat causes the air above to rise quickly. As the air rises, it creates winds that move faster and faster until they start to whirl round. When the winds are spinning very fast together, they become a hurricane.

Tornadoes

Tornadoes, or twisters, are tall funnels of wind that spin very fast. They are smaller and much faster than hurricanes. The main difference between hurricanes and tornadoes is that tornadoes form over land and hurricanes form over the sea. Tornadoes look like a rope of dark spinning winds coming down from a storm cloud. Tornadoes can travel far across land and they cause terrible damage to people's houses and crops.

*Scientists use **satellite** pictures like this to track hurricanes and warn people to move to a safe place if one is heading their way. The swirling cloud in the picture shows a hurricane forming over the sea.*

How do hurricanes move?

Once a hurricane has formed, it does not stay in one place. Hurricanes move in two ways. Like a spinning top, they spiral round a central point, called the hurricane's 'eye'. At the same time as they are spinning, they also move forwards or backwards at about 10 kilometres (6 miles) an hour across open water.

When do hurricanes die?

Because hurricanes get their energy from the heat that comes off warm ocean waters, they start to die out when they reach land because it is cooler there. They gradually slow down and eventually disappear. However, they can still cause terrible damage to coasts and they sometimes go on spinning quite a way inland.

Hurricanes around the world

Hurricanes have different names in different parts of the world. Hurricanes happen over the north Atlantic and Pacific Oceans. When similar storms happen in the Pacific and Indian Oceans they are called typhoons or cyclones. This world map shows you where hurricanes, cyclones, and typhoons usually start and the directions they usually travel.

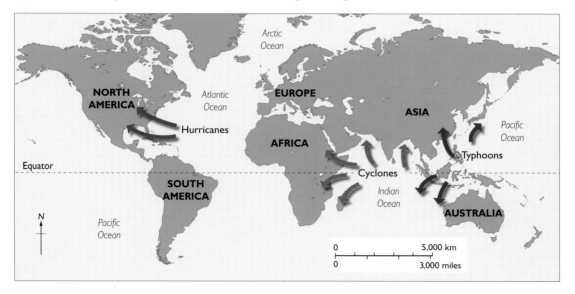

This map shows where tropical storms happen and what they are called in different parts of the world.

33

{case study} Hurricane Katrina

In August 2005, Hurricane Katrina became one of the most powerful hurricanes to hit the Gulf of Mexico and the USA in 50 years. Over 1,000 people were killed in the three states of Mississippi, Alabama, and Louisiana. Thousands of buildings and businesses were wrecked. One of the worst hit places was New Orleans.

Hurricane in New Orleans

As Hurricane Katrina swept through New Orleans, it destroyed buildings and tossed cars, trees, and debris across broken streets. But worse was to come. New Orleans lies below sea level and flood walls called levees keep seawater out. Many buildings were destroyed in New Orleans when the storm broke these levees. Water flooded almost the entire city. Thousands of people who had been unable to flee sheltered on rooftops or in the city's stadium. They were stranded for days without water or food, until rescue came. Workers soon began to pump out the water and repair the levees, but in late September Hurricane Rita brought more rain, and water poured over the patched-up defences to flood New Orleans once more.

Scenes of devastation were seen in New Orleans after Hurricane Katrina passed through.

Tracking a hurricane

Scientists tracked the route taken by Hurricane Katrina to help them predict where it might go next. They hoped to warn people it was coming. This map shows the exact route taken by Katrina during the time it blew over the Gulf coast in August 2005.

Hurricane Katrina began as a **low-pressure** weather system over **tropical** waters east of the Bahamas on 23 August. As it moved west, it strengthened into a hurricane. Winds travelling at the speed of 120 kilometres (75 miles) per hour left 100,000 homes and businesses without electricity. Worse was to come. As Hurricane Katrina swirled across the warm waters of the Gulf of Mexico on 26, 27, and 28 August, its winds grew even stronger. By 29 August, when Katrina reached the coast south of New Orleans, wind speeds were 200 kilometres (125 miles) per hour. Katrina carried on heading north over land, causing more and more destruction, until it died down to a mere storm on the morning of 30 August.

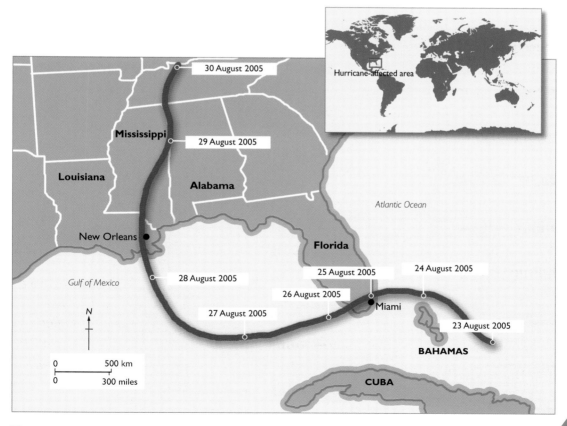

This map shows the route taken by Hurricane Katrina in August 2005.

{how is climate changing?}

Many scientists believe that the world's climate is changing and that around the world there has been a general increase in temperatures. Many people believe that this '**global warming**' is having a huge impact on the world's **climate**.

What causes global warming?

Many people believe global warming is caused by an increase in gases in the **atmosphere**. These gases contribute to what is known as the **greenhouse effect**. These gases come from the burning of **fossil fuels** such as oil, gas, coal, and wood. These are burned to create electricity in power stations or as fuel in our cars. The burning of giant forests to clear land for farming or building also causes these gases. These fumes are altering the amounts of gases in the atmosphere and gradually changing world temperatures.

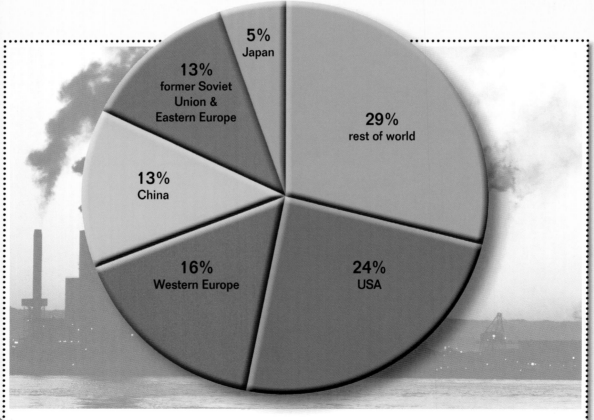

5%
Japan

13%
former Soviet
Union &
Eastern Europe

29%
rest of world

13%
China

16%
Western Europe

24%
USA

*This pie chart shows the amounts of greenhouse gases produced by different countries. Richer countries with more industries and big power stations that rely on fossil fuels produce more waste gas than **less-developed countries**.*

36

How the greenhouse effect works

The greenhouse gases in the atmosphere work like the glass in a greenhouse. They trap some of the warmth that comes to Earth from the Sun and stop it escaping back into space. This is important because it keeps our world at a temperature that allows us to live comfortably.

There are different greenhouse gases in the atmosphere, including **carbon dioxide** and methane. For thousands of years the amounts of these gases stayed about the same. However, in the last 100 years people have been releasing more greenhouse gases into the atmosphere. By cutting down forests they have made things worse. Trees absorb carbon dioxide. They use it in **photosynthesis**, the process by which they make food. Fewer trees mean there is more carbon dioxide in the air. With the amount of greenhouse gases in the atmosphere increasing, less and less heat can escape back into space. It becomes trapped at the Earth's surface and makes the world warmer.

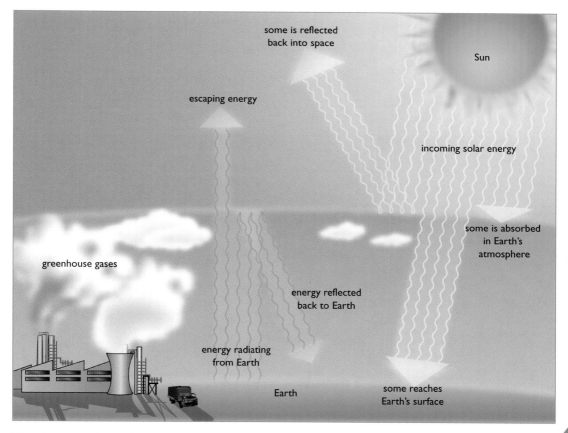

This diagram shows how greenhouse gases trap solar energy close to the Earth's surface.

{effects of global warming}

The global increase in temperature is about 0.6°C (33°F). It may not sound like much, but many people believe that this change in **climate** has already had an impact on our lives. In recent years, hurricanes, heatwaves, forest fires, floods, and **droughts** are just some of the weather hazards that have been blamed on **global warming**.

Extreme weather

Warm ocean temperatures create hurricanes so it is logical that a rise in temperature would be responsible for the fiercer and more frequent storms the world has been experiencing. Warmer seas also mean greater levels of **evaporation**, which mean fuller clouds that empty themselves suddenly, for example at **monsoons**, and cause floods. Some people believe that the increase in world temperatures is melting the huge ice sheets that cover the North and South Poles. This in turn causes the level of the sea around the world to rise. Many people believe this has led to worsening floods in coastal areas such as Bangladesh.

In long hot periods with little rain, plants become dry and fire can catch and spread quickly. In 2004 there were major forest fires in several countries across the world.

Climate change

Many people feel that the term 'climate change' is more helpful than 'global warming' because the effects of this gradual increase in temperature do not just mean the world will get hotter. As we have seen, the effects are much more complex than that. Some areas will be warmer, some will be cooler, some will be wetter, and many will be drier.

Hot topic

The issue of global warming is hotly debated around the world, both by scientists and by ordinary people. Some people think that freak weather events have always happened throughout history. Others believe that although this is true, extreme weather events are becoming more and more frequent and that the reason for this has to be global warming.

This young girl was rescued as floodwaters rose in the aftermath of Hurricane Katrina. Some people believe that climate change causes severe hurricanes.

{ case study }
Arctic ice

One of the most striking aspects of **global warming** is the melting of the **ice caps** (land permanently covered in ice) at the North and South Poles. At the North Pole, the Arctic temperatures are rising about eight times faster than almost anywhere else. White is a colour that reflects light and in the past sunlight has bounced off the ice caps back into space. As the ice caps begin to melt, however, the dark colours of the ocean or rock beneath them become visible. These dark colours absorb the heat and speed up the melting process.

Shrinking ice

The Arctic has always been covered in ice all year round, but if the ice continues to melt at its current rate, the area could be having ice-free summers within 50 or 60 years. This not only affects the plants and animals that live in the **tundra** there. Trapped under these layers of icy land are the remains of dead plants that have decayed very slowly over centuries. If all the ice melts, they will decay more quickly. As they decay, they will release **carbon dioxide** into the **atmosphere** and further increase global warming.

Polar bears under threat

Polar bears catch seals, their main food, from ledges of sea ice. As the sea ice melts it will be harder for polar bears to catch enough food to survive the Arctic winters. Some scientists fear the polar bear could be extinct (die out) in 100 years.

These two **satellite** pictures of the Arctic from above show how the North Pole has changed in the last 30 years. The top picture shows the North Pole region in 1979. The white area indicates the area of sea ice at that time. The bottom picture shows the same area of the North Pole in 2004. You can see that the area of sea ice has reduced.

{investigating global warming}

To understand **climate** change and to work out possible future weather patterns, scientists can study past weather patterns. We do not have written records of climates long ago, so they study parts of the natural world that were around in the past. These include ancient trees, coral, and mud from deep oceans and lakes. Scientists look at how these things developed at different times to work out what kinds of climates could have created these changes. Then they can put this information together with what they know about weather patterns today to see if they can create computer models for what will happen next.

Ice clues

Some scientists are looking deep under the ice for clues to the world's past climate. The scientists are part of EPICA, the European Project for Ice Coring in Antarctica. They are drilling a very deep hole into the ice and taking samples from different depths as they dig down.

Scientists store the ice samples they collect at −15 to −20 °C (−60 to −68 °F). The deepest ice they have retrieved is 3,350 metres (11,000 feet) deep and around 400,000 years old. By carefully studying air bubbles trapped inside these ancient pieces of ice, scientists can work out what the climate was like at the time the air was trapped.

Ice from the past

Scientists hope to use the ice samples to give us clues to the Earth's climate over the last 900,000 years. The deeper the ice from which the sample is taken, the older it is. For example, an ice sample from 3,200 metres (10,500 feet) below the surface would be from about 750,000 years ago. Scientists can tell what the temperature was at that time by looking at the weight of a substance called deuterium in the ice. If it is lighter than usual, then it means the climate was colder at that time. If it is heavy, they can say the Earth was warmer at that time. Scientists can tell how much **carbon dioxide**, one of the main gases in the **greenhouse effect**, was in the air from bubbles of gas trapped in the ice.

EPICA

The EPICA project is to last eight years and is made up of scientists from ten European countries. They are working in a place where temperatures can fall as low as –40 °C (–100 °F).

This EPICA scientist is shown with ice samples taken by drilling into ice that formed as layers of snow squashed together over thousands of years.

{the future}

No one can really say for certain what the future holds for the world's weather and **climate**. Although scientists agree the planet is warming up, they disagree about the causes of climate change. Also, it is impossible to predict how the Earth will be affected by these changes in the future.

What could happen?

If **global warming** continues, average temperatures around the world could go up by about 6 °C (11 °F) in the next 100 years. This would cause more **glaciers** and **ice caps** to melt. The rise in sea level this causes will bring many more floods at coasts. Some islands may be completely covered by water. If it gets too hot, rainforests might die. Without the rainforest trees that absorb some of the **carbon dioxide** in the air, this could make global warming even worse. Some scientists predict there will be more **drought** and that people will starve as crops die in the heat and water sources dry up.

What can be done?

People around the world are looking at ways of stopping global warming. They are using alternative ways of making electricity, that do not use **fossil fuels**, such as wind power. They are encouraging people to reduce the amount of electricity they use and trying to find ways of cutting down on the amount of carbon dioxide produced by cars. Some scientists even think that nature might help us. For example, if the amount of **water vapour** in the air increases in future, it might create thick cloud cover and shield us from some of the Sun's heat.

Scientists study the Sun to help find ways to stop global warming.

What we can do

There are lots of ways we can help reduce the amount of carbon dioxide we produce.

You can walk, cycle, or share lifts to school with friends to reduce the amount of air pollution pumped into the **atmosphere** by cars.

If you can, persuade your family to switch your electricity to a green tariff that uses renewable sources, such as wind power, instead of fossil fuels.

If you're cold, put a jumper on instead of turning up the heating. Turn lights and appliances like TVs or computers off when you leave a room.

It's important that governments make changes to reduce pollution but we can all do our bit to reduce the amount of greenhouse gases being pumped into the atmosphere.

{further resources}

Books

Global Warming, Fred Pearce (Dorling Kindersley, 2002)

Weather and Climate Change, L. Howell (Usborne Publishing Ltd, 2003)

Websites

You can explore the Internet to find out more about the weather. Websites can change, so if the links below no longer work, use a reliable search engine and type in keywords such as weather, clouds, climate, and global warming.

Find out about climate change at the BBC Weather Centre: www.bbc.co.uk/climate.

Find out more about saving energy at www.funenergy.org.uk/home.html.

At www.epa.gov the EPA global warming kids page has games and information about weather, climate, and global warming.

The www.fema.gov website has lots of information about weather disasters, games to play, and stories to read. It also has advice on how to be prepared for disasters if you live, for example, in a hurricane zone.

{glossary}

air pressure weight of air pressing on an area of the Earth's surface

atmosphere layers of air that surround planet Earth

biome large natural area with particular features that is home to a variety of plants and animals, such as tundra or rainforest

broadleaf woodland woodland with trees such as oak and beech, trees that lose their broad, flat leaves in winter

carbon dioxide invisible gas found in the Earth's atmosphere

climate general conditions of weather in an area

condensation when water turns from a gas (water vapour) to liquid water

coniferous forest forest containing conifer trees, trees with needle-like leaves such as pine and fir

drought long period of time without rain or with too little rain

Equator imaginary line around the centre of the Earth

evaporate what happens when liquid water changes into water vapour, a gas in the air

fossil fuels natural fuel such as oil, gas, or coal, which formed from the remains of living things trapped between layers of rock millions of years ago

glaciers incredibly slow-moving river of ice

global warming rise in temperatures across the world, caused by the greenhouse effect

greenhouse effect blanket of gases in the air that are trapping heat

high pressure areas of cool air are heavier than warm air. They are said to create areas of high pressure because they press down more heavily towards the Earth.

humidity moisture in the air

ice cap area permanently covered in ice, such as found at Poles

less-developed country country that is less industrialized, such as many countries in Africa, Asia, Latin America and the Caribbean, and Oceania.

low pressure areas of warm air are lighter than areas of cool air. They are said to create areas of low pressure because they press down less heavily towards the Earth.

meteorologists scientists who study the weather

monsoon rainy season in parts of Asia, Africa, and elsewhere

Northern Hemisphere the half of the Earth north of the Equator

orbit the curved route of an object, such as a planet or satellite, around a large planet

oxygen gas in the atmosphere that living things need to breathe in order to live

ozone layer a layer of gas in the atmosphere that absorbs harmful rays of sunlight

photosynthesis process by which plants make food in their leaves, using water, carbon dioxide from the air, and energy from sunlight

precipitation water falling from the sky in liquid or solid form, such as rain, snow, and hail

satellite object in space that sends out TV signals or takes photographs

Southern Hemisphere the half of the Earth south of the Equator

temperate climate with warm, dry summers and cool, wet winters

trade winds cool winds that blow from the north and south towards the Equator

tropical found in the tropics – countries around the Equator that have some of the hottest climates in the world

troposphere lowest layer of the atmosphere. It contains 90 percent of the air in the atmosphere. This is the part we live in and where our weather happens.

tundra area of frozen land where only a few kinds of plants, such as lichens and moss, can grow

water cycle the never-ending movement of water between the atmosphere and the Earth's surface

water vapour when water is a gas in the air. Steam from a boiling kettle is a kind of water vapour.

weather forecast information about what meteorologists predict the weather will be like in the next few days or weeks

weather forecaster person who gives weather forecasts, for example on radio or TV

{index}

Titles in the *Geography Focus* series include:

Hardback   1 74070 275 1
             978 1 74070 275 1

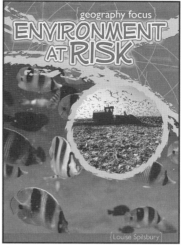

Hardback   1 74070 278 6
             978 1 74070 278 2

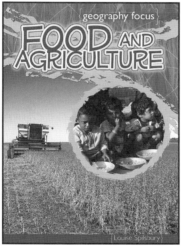

Hardback   1 74070 279 4
             978 1 74070 279 9

Hardback   1 74070 277 8
             978 1 74070 277 5

Hardback   1 74070 276 X
             978 1 74070 276 8

Hardback   1 74070 274 3
             978 1 74070 274 4

Find out about the other titles in this series on our website www.raintreepublishers.co.uk